the VEGG cookbook

Egg-Free Cooking Uncaged

by
ROCKY SHEPHEARD
SANDY DEFINO
And fans of The Vegg!

Design & Layout: Tracy Copes; tracy@daftgeneration.com

Published by
The Vegg
Pennsylvania, US
570.460.2139   rocky@thevegg.com

The Vegg is available at locations
listed at www.thevegg.com

CONTENTS

which came first
the cookbook or the Vegg?

I first started tinkering with a recipe for a vegan egg yolk in early 2010, inspired by an April Fool's Day post about a commercially available vegan fried egg. Early attempts were promising but didn't exactly replicate the texture and mouthfeel of a real egg yolk. Once I learned about molecular gastronomy and spherification techniques, The Vegg soon hatched. Luckily for you it is only a matter of adding water, and The Vegg is ready to be used in cooking and baking.

The Vegg had a lot of help leaving the nest. The main contributor was *Compassion Over Killing,* a visionary organization which continues to support and promote the Vegg. *A Well-Fed World* and *VegFund* also made generous donations towards launching the Vegg. I am so grateful to these wonderful organizations as well as to a myriad of other contributors, including family members, friends, and Vegg supporters worldwide.

As evidenced by this collection of recipes from international contributors, the Vegg's flock is growing! Kudos to all of the creative cooks who have embraced the Vegg and explored its varied applications. Your recipes help others take steps towards adopting an exciting and delicious, cruelty-free diet.

Please note: for reasons of consistency and trademark considerations, some recipes were modified from the original submissions. For questions regarding recipes, visit websites listed with recipes. I'd like to thank everyone who submitted and I hope you all enjoy The Vegg Cookbook!

Rocky

Foreward

**by Erica Meier
Executive Director of Compassion
Over Killing, Washington, D.C.**

Since the Vegg hit the market in 2012, people everywhere have been scrambling to try it and cook with it. This wonderful egg-free egg yolk replacer looks, smells, and even tastes like eggs – but without all the cruelty.

As you'll discover with this egg-citing new cookbook, the Vegg is a versatile product that's helping make vegan eating even easier – and tastier – than ever before. Now, you can easily whip up healthier (and hen-approved) French toast, tofu scramble, quiche, hollandaise sauce, desserts and so much more. It's also ideal as a liquid base when breading foods for frying, and you can even use it straight as a liquid "yolk" for dipping toast.

The Vegg and all the recipes in this cookbook are all-vegan, which is great news for the more than 280 million egg-laying hens in the U.S., most of whom spend their lives intensively confined inside barren wire cages. And since it's made using 100% plant-based ingredients, it's also 100% cholesterol-free, which makes it heart-healthy, too.

Compassion Over Killing is thrilled to introduce this cookbook to you, and to be a partner with The Vegg, helping get this product off the ground and into consumers' hands.

So get cracking in the kitchen today! Most importantly, be sure to share this book—and the amazing vegan meals you create—with your friends and family. Thank you for choosing compassion, and for helping create a kinder, cleaner, and healthier world for all animals.

EMeier

How To Spherify A Yolk

By: Rocky Shepheard
www.thevegg.com

Ingredients:

1 Tbs. prepared Vegg
1 tsp. calcium chloride beads dissolved in
1 cup of warm water
1 cup cold water (for rinse)

Note: You will need two small bowls, a spoon, and a drinking glass with a 2" diameter inside bottom

Pour a tsp. of calcium chloride solution into glass and swish around, making sure bottom and sides are coated. Pour out into sink.

Using a measuring cup, pour about 1/4" (approximately 1 Tbsp.) of prepared Vegg into glass (being very careful to not let it contact sides of glass). Let sit for 1 minute.

Fill standard sized non-measuring tsp. with calcium chloride solution. Near the top of the glass touch tip of spoon to inside of glass. Slowly lift spoon handle and let the solution drizzle down the side of the glass so as not to pour directly on yolk. Gently turn glass 45 degrees and repeat. Keep this up until top of yolk is covered with calcium chloride solution. Gently swirl the glass so the yolk spins around for 15 seconds.

Wait 2 minutes, then gently pour yolk into your hand so that the excess calcium chloride solution is poured into sink. Immediately put yolk into cold water bath for 2 minutes. Keep there until used.

TIP: If you prefer more disk shaped (realistic yolks) to spherical ones, just puncture the spherified yolk, bleed off some runny yolk and immediately submerge yolk into calcium chloride to reseal the puncture.

A little practice and you'll be making perfect vegan yolks!

World's Best (& most realistic) Vegan Fried Egg

By: Rocky Shepheard; www.thevegg.com

Ingredients:

2 cups water, divided
1 tsp. of sodium alginate
2 oz. firm tofu
1/4 tsp. of kala namak/black salt
1/2 tsp. calcium chloride
3-4 Tbs. of Vegg liquid or 1 spherified yolk
(see page 8)

Using a stick blender, blend sodium alginate with 1 cup of water until thick. Add 2 oz. firm tofu and blend for 1 minute. Add kala namak and blend for 1 more minute. Set aside.

In separate vessel, blend 1/2 tsp. calcium chloride with 1 cup of water until it is dissolved.

Spread out tofu mixture in dish, slightly larger than you want your fried egg to be. Leave an edge around tofu mixture. Pour the calcium chloride solution around the tofu mixture until it completely covers it (being careful not to pour it directly on the mixture as that will deform it).

After 1-2 minutes pour off the calcium chloride and pour cold water around the tofu mixture (being careful not to pour it directly on the mixture). Let it set for 2 minutes. If you like a thicker egg white leave calcium chloride on longer. If you like thinner, leave calcium chloride on for a shorter time.

Peel off the white and gently rinse in cold water to wash off any residual tofu mixture. Place in margarined frying pan.

Yolk options:

1. Super Easy: Add 3-4 Tbs. of Vegg liquid into pan while frying. This would make a broken yolk fried egg effect.

2. Requires Spherifed Yolk: Set spherified yolk on top of white for the last minute of frying.
NOTE: For a video on how to spherify a yolk go to https://www.youtube.com/watch?v=khpXdmJXddl

3. Extreme Type-A: If you want a more realistic looking fried egg, add a spherifed yolk on top of tofu mixture before pouring in the calcium chloride, so that the spherification holds the yolk to the white. (The calcium chloride must rise to slightly higher than the top of the yolk.)

Sodium alginate and calcium chloride can both be purchased on Amazon.

Veggs Benedict

By: Rocky Shepheard
www.thevegg.com

Ingredients:

1 spherified Vegg yolk (see page 8)
1/4 cup hollandaise sauce (see page 38)
bottom half toasted vegan english muffin
1 slice of vegan Canadian bacon
1 cup water
2 tsp. sodium alginate
1/2 tsp. kala namak/black salt
3 oz. firm tofu
1/4 tsp. calcium chloride beads dissolved
in 1 cup of warm water

Note: You will need a small glass ramekin with a curved bottom as a mold for the poached egg, a stick blender, and a tall vessel to blend ingredients.

Poached egg method:

Blend water and sodium alginate in tall vessel with stick blender until thick (approx. 1 min). Add in the tofu and kala namak and reblend until homogenous.

Put a tsp. of calcium chloride solution into ramekin and swish around. Pour it out into the sink.

Pour some tofu mixture in ramekin so that the entire inside of ramekin is coated. Pour the excess tofu mixture into the sink. Add spherified yolk.

With a spoon add a Tbsp. of calcium chloride solution on top and around yolk.

Pour more tofu mixture in ramekin just enough to covering the yolk. With a spoon add a Tbsp. of calcium chloride solution on top.

Place in fridge for 1-2 hours.

Fry vegan Canadian bacon until nicely carmelized and place on toasted and margarined english muffin.

With a thin, flexible spatula or something similar, separate yolk from edge of ramekin, going around the circumference of the ramekin, while continually pushing toward bottom, until yolk is free.

Place round side up on the vegan Canadian bacon. Pour hollandiase sauce over poached egg. Heat in microwave for 30-60 seconds and serve.

Salt and pepper as you like it.

Scrambled Veggs

By: Rocky Shepheard
www.thevegg.com

Ingredients:

2 gallons cold water
1 cup soy protein isolate
3 Tbs. Vegg powder
1 Tbs. nigari mixed in 1/4 cup hot water

Divide water equally into internal and external vessels of a large double boiler.

In the internal vessel, blend with a stick blender, soy protein isolate and Vegg, until it is dissolved.

Put the double boiler on high and heat (monitoring with a thermometer) until the contents of the internal pot reaches 175F.

Remove from heat. Stir three times and pour in the nigari solution. Cover for 1/2 hour.

Uncover and very gently (cannot stress this enough) scoop out curd with a fine mesh wire strainer and very gently place in a bowl that can go in the freezer.

Put in freezer overnight then thaw in microwave before frying.

Fry or microwave with vegan margarine and serve with salt, pepper and your favorite plant-based breakfast items.

Tangerine French Toast

By: Melissa Mullins; www.veganfling.com

Ingredients:
2 tsp. Vegg powder
3/4 cup water
3/4 cup almond milk
1 tangerine, juiced (about 1/4 cup juice)
a few drops vanilla
4-6 pieces bread, cut into thirds
vegan margarine

For garnish: powdered sugar, maple syrup,
tangerine slices

Mix Vegg powder, water, and almond milk in a blender. Pour this into a shallow dish. Stir in the tangerine juice and a few drops of vanilla.

Heat a skillet over medium-high heat and melt some vegan margarine. Dip both sides of bread into the liquid mixture. Fry the bread in the heated skillet, adding more vegan margarine as needed. Flip to cook both sides until golden brown.

Top with powdered sugar, maple syrup and tangerine segments.

Scrambled Tofu

By: Helen Rossiter
www.vegetarianrecipeclub.org.uk
www.lotsofnicethings.com

Ingredients:

2 tsp. of Vegg powder
1 cup water
sunflower or olive oil
8 oz. firm tofu
2 spring onions, finely chopped
salt and pepper

Blend together Vegg powder with the water and set aside.

Spray a hot frying pan with cooking spray, or use a tiny amount of oil or vegan margarine, then crumble in the tofu and add the spring onion. Cook for about 5 minutes, stirring, so it turns lightly golden.

Mix in the cup of Vegg and cook it in with the scrambled tofu until it reaches a consistency you like. The longer you cook it, the firmer it will become.

Season to taste and serve on toast, with brown or tomato sauce, or as part of a big vegan fried breakfast.

Vegg Pan-Crepes

By: Christa Bouchez
www.karmatarian.wordpress.com

Ingredients:
1/2 cup of prepared Vegg
(pre-mixed using plain almond milk)
1/2 cup organic all-purpose flour
3/4 cup + 2 Tbs. water
1+1/2 tsp. vanilla extract
1/8 tsp. + a pinch kala namak/black salt
cooking spray
organic powdered sugar
fruit for garnish/side
8" non-stick skillet

Premix The Vegg according to package directions, but use plain almond milk in place of water.

Take 1/2 cup of The Vegg mixture and add it to a bowl, then add remaining ingredients: flour, water, vanilla and black salt. Blend with a high speed blender until smooth.

Put this mixture in the refrigerator for 30 minutes.

Pre-heat an 8" non-stick skillet on medium-low heat.

Very lightly, spray the pan with cooking spray and pour a good grapefruit size portion of batter into the center of the pan. The trick is to get the right thickness. These are thicker than a crepe but not as thick as an omelet. You may have to play with it and you might even screw up the first one.

After pouring the batter, pick up the pan and rotate with your wrist to evenly distribute the batter to cover the entire bottom of the pan.

You will see the crepes start to shrink a bit, the edges will start to lift and the center will bubble a bit, and then you can flip it, BUT use your hands... do it fast, because they will be hot! I used a toothpick to delicately help me lift the edge a bit more, then I grabbed it with my fingertips using both hands and quickly flipped it over. You will see it bubble again. Cook 30 seconds, then gently fold over one side toward the middle and flip again to finish.

Move the finished pan-crepe to a plate and use a lid to keep it warm or a warming drawer etc... while you make your next one.

When all of the pan-crepes are finished being created, you will probably want to reheat them slightly. Sprinkle with powder sugar and serve. Don't forget the side of fruit!

**You simply cannot make this recipe without the black salt. This gives it the egg like flavor and color. You may even want to use more black salt than I suggest. It's all personal preference!

Vegg Omelet

By: Mimi Clark
www.veggourmet.wordpress.com

Ingredients:

1 Tbs. Vegg powder
1/2 cup non-dairy milk
1 box firm or extra firm tofu, drained
1 tsp. vegetable oil
2 tsp. vegan margarine

Fillings: scallion, bell pepper, mushrooms, spinach, vegan cheese, salsa, vegan sour cream, etc.

Combine Vegg and non-dairy milk in a blender or food processor until smooth; about 1 minute. Add drained tofu and oil. Blend or process until smooth; about 1 minute. Transfer mixture into a bowl or a measuring cup for easy pouring.

Heat 10" skillet on medium heat. Add vegan margarine and heat until melted.

Pour batter into skillet. Working quickly, spread batter over the entire pan using a spatula or the back of large spoon. Cook on medium heat for 10-15 minutes until the edges begin to set.

Scatter fillings of choice over half of the omelet. Slide a spatula under the entire perimeter of the omelet to loosen it. Using the largest spatula you have to prevent tearing the omelet, fold the unfilled side of the omelet over the filled side. The bottom of the omelet should be golden brown.

Cover the skillet with a large dinner plate turned upside down. With one hand on top of the plate, and one hand on the skillet handle, quickly flip the omelet onto the plate.

If the omelet is too soft for your liking, bake it in the oven for 10 minutes at 350F as you would a frittata.

Any Way You Want it Vegan Omelet

By: Kip Dorrell
www.messyvegetariancook.com

Serves 2

Ingredients:

6+1/2 oz. (half package) silken tofu
3 Tbs. soy flour
2 Tbs. tapioca starch
2 Tbs. prepared Vegg
1/4 tsp. black salt
salt and pepper
oil

Fillings:

(pre-grilled) asparagus, tomato, onion, peppers, seitan, etc.

Blend all of the ingredients in a blender or food processor.

Heat a skillet (I used cast iron) to medium heat and add a tsp. or two of oil to coat the pan.

Pour half of the eggy liquid into the center of the pan and use a spatula to spread it into a large circle (it won't flow naturally on its own).

Cook for 5 minutes or until most of the top side begins to dry out a bit.

Pile your desired filling on one half of the omelet and fold the other half over.

Press down ever so slightly with a spatula and leave to cook another minute or so before serving. Technically this is flip free because the omelet is mostly cooked by this point, but if you think it needs some time cooking on the other side then go for it!

Serve warm with salad or with other breakfast items.

Gluten Free French Toast

By: Amanda Newman
www.newandimproved.blogspot.com

Ingredients:

6 slices of gluten free, vegan bread
3 tsp. Vegg powder
1+1/4 cup soy, almond, or coconut milk
2 tsp. corn starch
1 tsp. vanilla
1/2 tsp. cinnamon
1 tsp. agave nectar
olive oil or canola oil spray
strawberries (optional for garnish)
powdered sugar (optional for garnish)

In a regular or hand blender, blend Vegg powder and 1/2 cup of the non-dairy milk. Make sure to scrape down the sides to get the mixture to blend well. Add in the cornstarch, vanilla, cinnamon, remaining non-dairy milk, and agave nectar and blend again. Place the mixture in a shallow bowl or pan, with enough room for two pieces of bread.

Place a skillet on medium heat and spray with olive oil or canola oil spray. While the skillet is heating, place two slices of bread into Vegg mixture and let it soak for about 5 minutes. When the pan is heated, place two pieces of bread in the skillet. Place two more pieces of bread into the mixture to soak. Turn the french toast in about 3 minutes when it is slightly browned. Cook until it is brown on the other side. Serve with sprinkled powdered sugar and sliced strawberries.

Buckwheat Waffles

By: Meggie and Ben Woodfield
www.meggieandben.blogspot.com

Makes 4-5 waffles

Ingredients:
1 cup buckwheat flour
1 cup spelt flour
2 tsp. baking powder
1/2 tsp. salt
1/8 tsp. nutmeg
1+3/4 cup non-dairy milk
2 Tbs. apple cider vinegar
1 tsp. Vegg powder
1/4 cup water
3 Tbs. vegan honey
2 Tbs. applesauce
oil or cooking spray

Combine buckwheat flour, spelt flour, baking powder, salt, and nutmeg in a bowl and whisk together.

In a blender, combine non-dairy milk and apple cider vinegar. Let sit for a few minutes. This will create a sort of buttermilk taste.

Add Vegg, water, vegan honey, and applesauce into a blender. Blend until smooth and Vegg is completely incorporated and there are no flakes left.

Grease waffle iron and heat. Add dry ingredients to wet ingredients and use a spatula to mix until just combined.

Pour some of the mixture into heated waffle maker and cook according to your waffle maker's instructions.

Vegg Nog Baked French Toast

By: Amanda Wolski
www.veganroadrunner.blogspot.com

Makes 4 servings

Ingredients:
16 slices cinnamon-raisin bread
2 cups vegan egg nog
1 tsp. Vegg blended with 1/4 cup water
1 tsp. ground nutmeg
1 tsp. ground cinnamon
maple syrup

Spray a 9"x11" baking dish with non-stick spray.

Cut the crusts off the bread. Make 2 layers of 8 slices each in the pan, making sure all slices are touching.

In a medium bowl, whisk together the nog, Vegg, nutmeg, and cinnamon.

Pour over the bread, covering evenly. Cover with plastic wrap and refrigerate overnight.

In the morning, preheat oven to 400F. Bake uncovered for 30-35 minutes or until the bread is dry to the touch.

Serve with maple syrup.

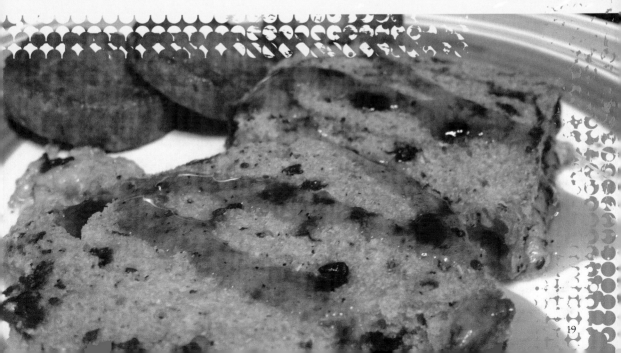

Lemon Poppyseed Pancakes

By: Meggie Woodfield
www.meggieandben.blogspot.com

Ingredients:

2 Tbs. sugar
2 Tbs. fresh lemon zest
2 cups whole wheat or white flour
2 tsp. baking powder
1 tsp. baking soda
1 tsp. salt
2 cups plain non-dairy milk
2 Tbs. apple cider vinegar
1 tsp. Vegg powder
1/4 cup water
2 tsp. vanilla
2 Tbs. fresh lemon juice
4 Tbs. vegan margarine, melted
2 Tbs. poppy seeds
maple syrup for serving

In a small bowl combine granulated sugar and lemon zest. Rub together with your fingers until sugar is fragrant. Set aside.

In a large bowl, whisk together flour, baking powder, baking soda, and salt. Stir in the lemon sugar. Set aside.

In a separate bowl, whisk together non-dairy milk and apple cider vinegar to make 'buttermilk.' Let sit for 5 minutes.

In a blender, combine vinegar, 'buttermilk', Vegg, water, vanilla, lemon juice, and melted margarine until the mixture is smooth and there are no flakes remaining. Pour the wet ingredients all at once into the dry ingredients. Add the poppy seeds and stir to combine. If a few lumps remain, don't worry about it. Let the batter rest for 10 minutes while your griddle/pan heats.

Grease the griddle or pan over medium heat. Dollop batter onto hot griddle or pan. For small pancakes, use about 2 Tbs. for each pancake. For larger pancakes, use about 1/4 cup of batter. Cook until golden brown on the bottom and bubbling on top. Flip once and cook until golden brown on each side.

Place cooked pancakes on an oven-proof plate and place in a warm (about 150F) oven until all pancakes are cooked and ready to serve. Serve with maple syrup.

Sweet (or Savory) Crepes

By: Sandy DeFino
www.thevegg.com

Ingredients:

1/4 cup prepared Vegg
1/2 cup non-dairy milk
1/8 cup water
1/2 cup flour
1 Tbs. melted vegan margarine

Combine Vegg, non-dairy milk and water. Whisk in flour, then melted margarine.

Ladle 1/4-1/2 cup of batter into a heated, greased pan. You want a thin layer. The amount of batter you use per crepe will depend on the size of your pan.

Cook on medium heat for approximately 2 minutes. When the edges start to curl, loosen all around the edges, and flip carefully. The bigger your crepe, the harder it is to flip. Cook an additional minute on the second side.

Respray or grease the pan after every 1-2 crepes.

Fill with fruit and top with whipped cream—or eat them anyway you want!

For a sweeter crepe, add 1/2 Tbs. sweetener to the batter.

For a more savory crepe, add dried or fresh herbs to the batter, and a pinch of salt.

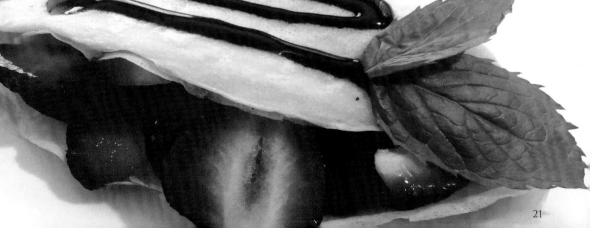

Vegg French Toast

By: Melissa Cacioppo
www.jerseycityvegan.com

Ingredients:

2 tsp. Vegg powder
1/2 cup water
1/2 cup non-dairy milk
1/4 tsp. vanilla
cinnamon to taste (a few shakes)
your favorite bread

Combine Vegg and water in a blender until smooth (10-15 seconds)

In a separate, shallow bowl, combine non-dairy milk, vanilla, and cinnamon and mix thoroughly. Add Vegg mixture.

Coat both sides of your favorite kind of bread with the french toast mixture.

Coat your pan with your favorite vegan margarine on medium-high and place your french toast in the pan to cook.

Cook for a few minutes on each side, until golden brown.

Serve with real maple syrup and your favorite vegan sausage.

Tofu Vegg Omelet

By: Brianna Clark-Grogan
www.veganfeastkitchen.blogspot.com

Makes 5 to 6 omelets
Use an 8"-10" nonstick skillet for this recipe.
If you don't have nonstick, use well-seasoned
cast iron or hard-anodized, but you may need a
little more fat for cooking.

Ingredients:

3/4 cup water
1+1/2 Tbs. Vegg powder
12.3 oz. box extra-firm silken tofu,
drained and crumbled
4+1/2 Tbs. chickpea flour
2 Tbs. tapioca flour
3/4 tsp. baking powder
1/2 tsp. salt
per omelet you will need 1 tsp. oil
or vegan margarine

Fillings: vegan cheese, sautéed mushrooms,
red pepper strips, etc. *Use your imagination but*
have your filling ready and kept warm before you
begin cooking the omelets, because they cook
quickly.

In a blender, process the water and Vegg powder
until well mixed and a bit gloppy-looking. Add
the remaining ingredients and blend until smooth.
Scrape into a bowl or measuring pitcher.

Heat your omelet pan over medium-low heat with
the oil or vegan margarine.

Use from 1/3 cup to 1/2 cup of batter per omelet,
depending on how large you want them to be.
Scoop it into the center of the pan. Using the
back of a spoon in a circular motion, try to evenly
spread the batter outwards to make a circle that's
fairly thin, but with no holes. Turn the heat up to
high, cover and let cook for a couple of minutes,
or until the top is set and dry and the bottom is
golden and a bit crispy.

Turn the heat down to low again and place
some of your filling and vegan cheese (if you
are using it) over one half of the circle and use
the spatula to fold the other half over the filling.
Cover the pan again and leave for a minute or
two to melt the cheese. Slide onto a warm plate
and repeat with the remaining batter.

Leftover omelet can be folded or rolled like
a crepe and refrigerated. It can be quickly
microwaved and filled for another meal, or
chopped (while cold) and used in fried rice.

Make a well in the center of the flour and pour in the liquid. Mix in with a wooden spoon before adding the lukewarm water. Stir until the flour and liquid combine to form a dough.

Knead on a lightly floured surface for 10 minutes Place in an oiled mixing bowl, cover with a clean tea towel and place somewhere warm to rise for one hour, until doubled in size.

Remove dough from the bowl and lightly knead again, before rolling into a sausage shape and dividing into 12 pieces. Roll each piece into a ball in your hands.

Press your thumb into the center of each ball to make a hole. Insert a second finger and roll both fingers around each other to widen the gap, stretching into a bagel shape.

Pre-heat your oven to 400F.

Bring a large saucepan of salted water to a boil.

Drop the bagels in and let them bob around on the top for around 30-40 seconds, turning with a slotted spoon.

As you remove each bagel from the water, shake off any water and place them on an oiled baking tray. Brush with a little oil.

Bake for 20-25 minutes until golden brown. When they are cooked, place on a wire rack to cool.

Either serve as they are, or cut them in half, lightly toast and serve with vegan margarine or vegan cream cheese.

Bristol-Style Bagels

By: Helen Rossiter
www.vegetarianrecipeclub.org.uk
www.lotsofnicethings.com

Makes 12 small bagels
Preparation/cooking time 1 hour 40 minutes

Ingredients:
3 cups/1lb. strong white bread flour
1/2 tsp. salt
1 packet easy-blend instant yeast
1/4 cup prepared Vegg
1 tsp. brown sugar or agave syrup
2 tsp. olive oil
7 fl. oz. lukewarm water

Sift flour into a large mixing bowl and mix in the salt and yeast.

Add sugar or syrup to olive oil and blended Vegg and mix.

Pan de Mallorca

By: Dynise Balcavage
www.urbanvegan.net

Makes 6 rolls

Ingredients:
1/2 cup non-dairy milk
1/2 cup water
1+1/2 tsp. yeast
3 cups white flour, divided
2/3 cup sugar
1/4 cup prepared Vegg
1 tsp. vanilla
a pinch of salt
1 stick vegan margarine, melted, divided in half (more if desired)
About 1/4 cup powdered sugar, for dusting

Warm non-dairy milk and water in microwave or saucepan until it reaches wrist temperature.

Using a mixer, with whisk blade, add yeast, 1 cup flour, and sugar to non-dairy milk and water.

Cover and let rise for an hour in a draft-free place. The mixture will be foamy and smell slightly yeasty.

Add the rest of the flour, Vegg, vanilla, salt, and half the melted vegan margarine.

Once again, cover and let rise until doubled, about 45 minutes to 1 hour.

On a floured surface, roll or press dough out into a rectangle then roll rectangle toward you into a log, similar to how you form cinnamon rolls.

Cut log into 6 pieces. Place them on oiled cookie sheet, then gently brush with the remaining vegan margarine.

Preheat the oven to 375F.

Let the rolls rise for about 30 minutes. If you want, you can brush once more with melted vegan margarine after this rise, then bake for 15-20 minutes or until golden.

Dust generously with powdered sugar just before serving.

the
main
dish.

Vegan Sagaponack Corn Pudding

By: Michelle Thiele
www.michellestinykitchen.blogspot.com

*Note: this makes a huge casserole,
so feel free to cut the recipe in half.*

Ingredients:

6 Tbs. vegan margarine
5 cups yellow corn kernels
1 cup chopped yellow onion
2 tsp. of Vegg powder blended with 1/2 cup
water (about 4-6 yolks)
1+1/4 cups almond or non-dairy milk
1/2 cup yellow cornmeal
1 cup firm tofu, drained, crumbled
and firmly packed
3 Tbs. chopped fresh basil
1 Tbs. sugar
salt and freshly ground pepper, to taste
3/4 cup non-dairy cheddar, + extra to
sprinkle on top

Preheat the oven to 375F. Grease the inside of an 8-10 cup baking dish.

Melt the margarine in a very large saute pan and saute the corn and onion over medium-high heat for 4 minutes. Cool slightly.

Whisk together Vegg and non-dairy milk in a large bowl. Slowly whisk in the cornmeal and then the tofu. Add the basil, sugar, salt, and pepper. Add the cooked corn mixture and vegan cheddar, and then pour into the baking dish. Sprinkle the top with more vegan cheddar

Place the dish in a larger pan and fill the pan 1/2 way up the sides of the dish with hot tap water. Bake the pudding for 40-45 minutes until the top begins to brown and a knife inserted in the center comes out clean. Serve warm.

This pudding is especially great for large gatherings, because the final texture and taste are best when it is prepared in advance and allowed to set in the refrigerator overnight.

Artichoke Tomato Quiche

By: Liz Whitaker
www.veganfoodrocks.blogspot.com

Ingredients:

1+1/4 tsp. Vegg powder
1+1/2 Tbs. cornstarch
1/4 cup water
1 pkg. firm tofu drained and pressed
a pinch or two of dried sage
1/2 Tbs. of dried rosemary, crushed
salt and pepper to taste
1 can of artichoke hearts roughly chopped,
drained and squeezed to remove extra liquid
12-14 grape tomatoes, quartered
6-8 sheets phyllo dough
3 Tbs. of melted vegan margarine or olive oil

Preheat oven to 350F. While the oven heats up, place a sheet of phyllo dough on the counter, brush with melted vegan margarine and place another sheet directly on top.

Repeat until you have used all the dough.

Gently pick up the pile of dough and place it over the pie plate and using your fingers, push it into place, getting all around the bottom. Give the bottom a few stabs with a fork or knife, otherwise it will puff up a bunch while cooking.

Cook crust for 8-10 minutes and start preparing filling.

In a blender, mix water, Vegg powder and cornstarch.

In a food processor crumble the tofu, add the spices and Vegg mixture. Pulse until smooth and completely mixed. Pour into a bowl and mix in the chopped artichoke and tomato.

Once phyllo crust is pre-baked, pour in the filling and bake for 35-40 minutes.

Veggy Burger

By: Rocky Shepheard/Sandy DeFino
www.thevegg.com

Ingredients:
1 15.5 oz. can of black beans
1/4 cup diced red pepper
1 small carrot, grated
1 tsp. vegan worcestershire sauce
1/8 cup barbeque sauce
1/4 cup vital wheat gluten
1/4 cup binding mix*
1/4 cup bread crumbs
salt and pepper to taste

*Binding Mix:
1 cup water
2 tsp. sodium alginate
1 Tbs. Vegg powder

Directions for Binding Mix: Blend all ingredients for binding mix with a stick blender in a tall vessel. (set aside, you will not use all of it.)

Burger Directions: Drain beans and place in a large bowl. Mash coarsely.

Mix in red pepper, carrot, worcestershire sauce, barbeque sauce and a quarter cup of binding mix. Then add in bread crumbs.

Salt and pepper as desired. Finally mix in vital wheat gluten.

Form mixture into patties. Microwave patties for 4 minutes. (Texture will be softer if you skip this step.)

Pan fry in a very small amount of oil or vegan margarine.

Broccoli Quiche

By: Helen Rossiter
www.vegetarianrecipeclub.org.uk
www.lotsofnicethings.com

Serves 4-6
Time: 1 hour approximately

Ingredients:

4 tsp. Vegg powder
1 cup water
7 oz. silken tofu
7 oz. broccoli, broken into florets
1 Tbs. olive oil
1 small onion, chopped
1 clove garlic, crushed
4 large sundried tomatoes, sliced
2 oz. vegan cheese
salt and pepper

Pastry*

1/2 cup plain flour
a pinch of salt
1/4 cup vegan margarine
2-3 Tbs. cold water
You could also use a vegan ready-made crust.

Preheat the oven to 400F.

Make the pastry by sifting the flour into a mixing bowl then rubbing in the vegan margarine and salt. Add the water gradually, bringing the dough together with a wooden spoon. Press it down in the bowl with your fist so all the flour is incorporated

Flour a rolling pin and your worktop and roll out the pastry into a large thin round.

Grease a 10" pop-bottom flan dish and lay the pastry into it. Press it gently round the edge and sides so it fits then trim off any excess dough.

Bake the pastry for about 5 minutes in the oven, so it won't go soggy when the filling is added. Remove from the oven and set aside.

Meanwhile, steam or boil the broccoli for just a few minutes, so it retains a nice crunch.

In a blender, blend Vegg flakes/powder with the water, then put into a mixing bowl with the tofu and blend again. Salt and pepper to taste. Fry the onions and garlic in the oil for 5 minutes, until they are soft.

To assemble the quiche, arrange the broccoli, onion and garlic in the pastry case, spoon in the tofu/Vegg mix over the top and mix it in well. Sprinkle on the grated vegan cheese and sun-dried tomatoes. Top with salt and pepper to taste.

Bake the quiche for around 45 minutes, until it is cooked and the filling has set. Test this by inserting a knife into the center. Cook for longer if required. Serve hot or cold, delicious with salad.

Delicious Low-Fat Veggiennaise

By: Brianna Clark-Grogan
www.veganfeastkitchen.blogspot.com

Ingredients: Mix A:

1 cup non-dairy milk
2-4 Tbs. extra-virgin olive oil,
hemp oil or flaxseed oil (or a mix)
2 Tbs. apple cider, plain rice vinegar, or
white wine vinegar, or lemon juice
1+1/2 tsp. salt
1 tsp. Vegg powder
1/4-3/4 tsp. dry mustard (to taste)

Ingredients: Mix B:

1/2 cup + 2 Tbs. cold water
1/2 tsp. agar powder
3+1/2 Tbs. cornstarch or wheat starch
(do not substitute other starches!)
1/16 tsp. xanthan gum or guar gum

Place all of the Mix A ingredients into your blender or food processor and set aside.

In a small saucepan or microwave-proof bowl, mix together the water and agar from Mix B, and let sit for a few minutes. Add the cornstarch and whisk well. If making on the stovetop, stir constantly over high heat until thick and translucent-not white. Microwave option: Use the microwave-proof bowl for the mixture, and microwave on 100% power for 30 seconds. Whisk. Repeat this about 3 times, or until thick and translucent.

Tip: #1: If you don't cook this thoroughly, the mayo won't thicken properly.

Tip #2: Make sure to scrape the bottom of the pot or bowl with the whisk, so that no cornstarch gets left at the bottom.

Scrape the cooked Mix B into Mix A. Quickly add the xanthan or guar gum. Blend until the mixture is white, frothy and emulsified (no oil globules).

Pour into a clean pint jar, cover and refrigerate for several hours, until it is set. It should be firm enough to stand a knife up in.

Keep refrigerated. Will keep for about 2 weeks.

**Do you prefer a well-known "tangier" version of a mayo-like dressing? Use 1/2-1 tsp. mustard powder, and add 1 Tbs. lemon juice and 1 Tbs. organic sugar or agave nectar to "Mix A" (sugar levels in this type of recipe vary, so start with this and then let your taste dictate).

Vietnamese Pancakes with Veggies & Herbs

By: Nancy Montuori Stein
www.ordinaryvegan.net

Ingredients Pancakes:

1+1/2 cups rice flour
1/4 cup of water with 2 tsp. Vegg blended
1/2 tsp. salt
1 tsp. ground turmeric
1+3/4 cups canned coconut milk
a little veggie or sunflower oil

Sauce:

2+1/2 Tbs. lime juice
1+1/2 Tbs. toasted sesame oil
1 Tbs. brown sugar
1 Tbs. rice wine vinegar
1 Tbs. sweet soy sauce
2 tsp. grated fresh ginger
1 fresh red chile, finely chopped
1 garlic clove, crushed
1/2 tsp. salt

Fillings:

1 large carrot, peeled and shredded
2 radishes, shredded
4 green onions, sliced and cut on an angle
1 fresh green chile, seeded, sliced into strips
1+1/2 cups snow peas, sliced into strips
1 cup shredded cilantro leaves
2/3 cup shredded thai basil leaves
1/4 cup shredded mint leaves
1 cup mung bean sprouts
1 cup enoki mushrooms (optional)

Sauce: Just whisk together all the ingredients.

Pancakes: Blend the rice flour, Vegg mixture, salt and turmeric in a large bowl. Slowly add the coconut milk, whisking well to avoid any lumps. You want a thinnish pancake batter. Add more water or coconut milk if necessary.

Heat up a large non-stick frying pan, making sure it doesn't get too hot. Add a tiny amount of oil.

Pour in a couple of scoops of the batter, making a medium pancake. Once the underside is golden brown, turn the pancake over and cook the other side. Remove from the pan and keep warm while you make the other pancakes.

Place a warm pancake on each serving plate and pile vegetables and herbs over half of it. Drizzle the vegetables with some sauce and fold the other half of the pancake over them. Spoon some more sauce on top and serve. I like to sprinkle a little extra brown sugar over the top before I spoon the sauce on. Enjoy!

Cheese-Stuffed Ravioli in White Wine Sauce

By: Erin Wysocarski
www.olivesfordinner.com

Ingredients: *(to make 36 raviolis)*

Filling:
1 can of full-fat coconut milk
1 tsp. coconut vinegar
1/2 tsp. salt
1+1/2 tsp. powdered agar
2 Tbs. nutritional yeast
1/2 cup of vegan mozzarella shreds
a pinch of dried nutmeg
a few dashes of fresh-cracked pepper

*Broth: (to use in the sauce)
4 Tbs. olive oil
2 large onions, roughly diced
10 oz. white mushrooms, quartered
1 Tbs. large-crystal salt
4 cups water

Dough:
3 tsp. of Vegg powder
6 tsp. powdered egg replacer
3/4 cup water
2 cups "00" flour

Sauce:
1 Tbs. vegan margarine
1 Tbs. olive oil
1/2 cup bella mushrooms, thinly sliced
2 shallots, minced
4 cloves garlic, minced
3/4 cup dry white wine
1 cup onion-mushroom broth*
1/2 tsp. salt
1/4 cup chopped walnuts
3 Tbs. chopped fresh parsley

To make the filling: Bring the coconut milk, vinegar, salt and agar powder to a small boil in a saucepan. Remove from the heat and stir in the nutritional yeast. Pour into a glass pyrex dish to gel in the refrigerator for about an hour.

Place the gelled cheese into a bowl and mash well with a fork. Add in the vegan shreds and stir well to combine. Add in the pepper and nutmeg. Place back into the refrigerator.

To make the broth: Place all of the broth ingredients, except water into a large pot and saute for about 25 minutes over medium heat, stirring frequently. Increase the heat to high, then add in the 4 cups of water. Bring to a boil, then immediately dial the heat back down to medium-low, and simmer for about an hour. Once it is cooled, squeeze the cooked vegetables over a bowl, then discard. Then strain the rest of the broth. Transfer to a container and place into the refrigerator.

To make the pasta dough: Place Vegg, powdered egg replacer and water into a mixer or blender. Combine at highest setting.

Pour out the 2 cups of flour into a pile on your countertop. Make a well in the center, then add half of the Vegg mixture. Knead it a bit, then add the rest of the Vegg mixture. The dough should be soft and silky, and should not stick to your fingers. Add a few splashes of water or extra flour as needed to achieve this consistency.

Separate the dough into four pieces and roll them into balls. Flatten them out slightly, place on a cutting board and drape a damp towel over it. Let dough rest for 30-45 minutes.

To roll out your pasta: Flour your work area then flatten a piece of dough using a rolling pin. Try to get it as thin as possible, and apply consistent pressure to ensure that the thickness of the pasta is consistent throughout.

To make the raviolis: *I used a ravioli mold.*

Flour the mold. Drape a piece of the rolled-out pasta over it. Place the plastic piece over the top to create little dips to place your cheese into. Remove it.

Fill the dips with your cheese mixture, about a tsp. full. I placed a parsley leaf in first.

Next, roll out another piece of pasta, then drape it over the top. Using your fingers, gently press down all over the top to get rid of any air in between the cheese and pasta.

Take a rolling pin and roll it around the edges only (I found it easier to do this than to go over the entire top portion).

Remove the dough carefully from around the edges. Then, slowly turn it upside-down and gently push out the pasta with your fingers. Keep it really close to the counter. Then cut them apart, using a pasta wheel.

Let them dry on a rack for about an hour.

Place the raviolis in a single layer in a plastic bag. Place onto a cutting board for support, then place them into the freezer until ready to use.

When you are ready to make some of the pasta, remove from the freezer to slightly thaw for about 20 minutes before boiling.

To make your white wine sauce: Place the vegan margarine and olive oil into a skillet over medium heat. Add in the mushrooms, and saute for about 5 minutes. Then add in the shallots and garlic. Saute until softened, for 2-3 minutes more.

Turn the heat up to high, then add in the white wine. Allow to sizzle for a few minutes, then add in the broth and salt and allow to reduce by half. Then throw in the walnuts for about a minute. Remove from the heat and stir in the parsley.

To boil the pasta: bring plenty of salted water to a boil in a large pot. Add only 4-5 pieces of ravioli at a time, and boil for only a few minutes, until the pasta rises to the top of the pot.

Serve the pasta piping hot with some of the white wine wine sauce on top.

Eggless Salad

By: Stacy Di-Lin
www.veganfatty.com

Ingredients:
2 12 oz. blocks extra firm tofu
2 Tbs. prepared Vegg
1 cup vegan mayonnaise
2 tsp. Dijon mustard
1 tsp. dry mustard
1/4 tsp. kala namak/black salt
1/2 tsp. black pepper

Remove as much of the liquid as possible from the tofu. The tofu should be so dry that it begins to crumble. Each block of tofu should be pressed for at least four hours, if not overnight. The salad will be watery if you don't take the time to dry the tofu. When pressed, crumble the tofu with your fingers.

Mix 1 Tbs. of dry Vegg powder with 1 cup of water in a high speed blender. Do not hand mix, it must be blended.

Add 2 Tbs. (only) of Vegg mixture to the vegan mayonnaise, and mix together. Then add the Dijon and dry mustard, black salt, and pepper and mix well. Add crumbled tofu and fold into wet ingredients.

Spaetzle German Vegg Noodle

By: Ellen Graham
www.dontfearthevegan.com

Ingredients:

2/3 cup water + 3/4 cup water
1 Tbs. Vegg powder
1/2 Tbs. cornstarch
1+3/4 cups unbleached flour
1/2 cup garbanzo bean flour
1 tsp. Himalayan salt (fine grind)
3 Tbs. vegan margarine

Mix together Vegg and cornstarch so that they are well blended. Add 2/3 cup water and blend with either an immersion or regular blender.

In a large bowl mix together both flours and salt. Create a well in the center of the flour mixture. Add remaining water to Vegg mix, then pour into the well in the center of the flour. Mix by hand until smooth. Mixture will be thicker than pancake batter.

In a large pot bring 3 quarts of water to a boil. In small batches press noodles into boiling water using a strainer or potato ricer and cook for about 5 minutes, until they come to the top. Remove from water and strain. Repeat until you have cooked all of the dough.

Once noodles have cooled, melt vegan margarine in a frying pan over medium heat and fry until for a couple of minutes. Serve.

Vegan Hollandaise Sauce

By: Cobi Kim; www.veggietorials.com

Ingredients:

3 Tbs. Vegg powder
1/4 cup melted vegan margarine
(If using a microwave, do not over heat
or it will separate. Microwave in 20
second increments and watch closely).
1 tsp. Dijon mustard
1 tsp. hot sauce
juice of 1 lemon
1+1/2 cups hot water

Combine first 5 ingredients in a food processor or blender. Add 1+1/2 cups water. You may need to add more water later to reach your desired consistency. Blend on high speed until smooth and creamy. Add more water as needed if you prefer a thinner sauce.

Use immediately, or the mixture will start to gel slightly. Store covered in the refrigerator for up to a day.

Vegan Egg Rolls

By: Loryn Irwin
www.vegangoodness.com

Ingredients:
1 Tbs. Vegg powder
3/4 cup cold water
1/4 tsp. salt
7/8 cup flour
peanut oil for cooking

Wisk together everything but oil.

Heat nonstick pan to high heat, then lower to low once hot. Add oil to pan.

Scoop in 1/4 cup of flour mixture. Immediately spread out mixture to a thin layer. In under a minute the edges will begin to curl and the wrapper is done.

Place on paper towel to cool.

Once cool, fill with filling and wrap. (I used cabbage, carrots, scallions, bean sprouts and fresh ginger lightly sautéed with a dash of soy sauce).

You can then fry or bake eggrolls. I sprayed mine with oil and baked on 400F until browned.

Homemade Vegg Pasta

By: Caitlin Galer-Unti
www.theveganword.com

Makes 2 servings

Ingredients:
1/4 cup prepared Vegg
2 cups of pasta flour

Form a well in the flour and pour in the blended Vegg yolk.

Mix the flour and Vegg together with a fork, adding more water if needed, and knead until the dough is thick and slightly stretchy.

Roll out the dough as thin as desired, and cut into the desired shape (very thin strips for linguine, wider strips for pappardelle, etc.)

*Tip: **Fresh pasta cooks faster than dried pasta, so it will only need 3 or 4 minutes in boiling water. Add the fresh pasta strips to boiling water. Once they rise to the top and float, they are done.*

Jalapeño Poppers

By: Kelly Cavalier
www.threeandahalfvegans.blogspot.com

Ingredients:
1 Tbs. Vegg powder
1/2 cup soy milk
1+1/2 cups panko bread crumbs
2 tsp. garlic powder
2 tsp. onion powder
1 tsp. Italian seasoning
salt and pepper
1 cup all-purpose flour
8 jalapeño peppers, halved, seeds
and ribs removed
1 pkg. vegan cream cheese
oil for frying

Using a blender, combine Vegg powder and soy milk and blend until well mixed and thick. Pour into a small bowl and set aside.

Combine panko with the spices/seasonings in another small bowl, set aside.

Put flour into another small bowl and set aside.

Using a small spoon, fill the jalapeños with the cream cheese. To bread them, first roll each popper in the flour, dip in Vegg yolk mixture, then press and roll each popper in the panko bread crumbs until they are completely covered. Place on a plate until you are ready to fry them.

Heat your oil in a pot or pan. Only fill with enough oil so the poppers are about half covered in oil. Fry them in batches of 4-6 depending on the size of the pot/pan you are frying in until golden brown, flipping as you start to see the edges brown.

Remove from the oil and place on a paper towel on a cooling rack to get some of the oil off. Serve and enjoy!

Tofu & Pajeon (Scallion) Pancake

By: Cobi Kim
www.veggietorials.com

Prep: 15 minutes | Cook: 1 hour
Makes 4 servings

Ingredients for baked tofu and marinade:
1 block firm or extra firm tofu, pressed
1/3 cup + 2 Tbs. soy sauce
4 Tbs. liquid cane sugar syrup or agave
4 cloves garlic, minced
1 Tbs. fresh ginger, minced
3 Tbs. green onions, finely chopped
2 Tbs. mirin
1 Tbs. rice vinegar
1 Tbs. sesame oil
1 Tbs. roasted sesame seeds
half korean pear, grated (optional)
When using the pear, place with other marinade ingredients in a blender, and blend until smooth.

For the scallion pancake:
15 thin green onions, cut into 5" pieces
1/2 cup flour
1/2 cup water
1/2 tsp. baking soda
1 tsp. sugar
1 tsp. miso
2 Tbs. Vegg, premixed
2 Tbs. coconut oil

For the Tofu: Drain tofu. Remove excess water with a tofu press or wrap block of tofu between two kitchen towels and place heavy books on top for about 20 minutes. Slice the tofu block in half so that each piece is about 1" thick. This process will allow the marinade to be easily absorbed.

Mix all the marinade ingredients together in a small bowl. Adjust seasoning and add black pepper to taste. Place the tofu in a rimmed dish and pour the marinade on top. Refrigerate and marinate for at least 2 hours, overnight is best.

Preheat oven to 400F. Line a baking sheet with parchment paper. Place tofu in the middle of the sheet and bake for an hour. (Flip the tofu over after 30 minutes to cook and brown evenly.) Remove from oven and cool slightly before slicing.

For the scallion pancake: Mix together all the pancake ingredients (except the oil and green onions) to create the batter. Heat 1 Tbs. coconut oil over high heat and place half of the scallions in even layer in a nonstick pan. Pour just enough batter over the scallions to cover them. Cook for about 2+1/2 minutes, until the edges start to form bubbles. Flip the pancake, reduce heat to medium high and cook for an additional 3 minutes. Serve with gochujang sauce if you like it spicy.

Letcho

By: Monika Sedlarova
www.monikasedlarova.com

Makes 4 servings

Ingredients:

2 Tbs. oil
2 large onions
6 bell peppers
8 medium tomatoes
2 tsp. Vegg powder
1/2 cup water
salt and pepper to taste

Chop the onions into small pieces and saute over not too high heat in a pan with oil.

Cut the peppers into strips and add them to the pan. Salt and pepper to taste.

Once the peppers are soft, add the chopped tomatoes. Lower heat and cook until tomatoes begin to soften.

Blend 2 tsp. of Vegg with 1/2 cup of water and add to pan. Cook for another 4-6 minutes.

Serve with bread.

Linguine alla Carbonara

By: Hannah Kaminsky
www.bittersweetblog.wordpress.com

Makes 2-4 Servings

Ingredients:

1/2 lb. linguine
2 Tbs. melted vegan margarine or oil
1 small yellow onion, finely diced
2 cloves garlic, finely minced
1 cup vegetable stock
1/2 cup plain vegan creamer
1 Tbs. brown rice miso paste
1/4 tsp. ground black pepper
1 Tbs. Vegg powder
fresh parsley, chopped
vegan bacon

Cook and drain your pasta according to the directions on the box; set aside.

In a medium skillet or saucepan, heat the margarine or oil over medium heat. Add in the diced onion and saute for about 3 minutes, until softened. Toss in the garlic next, and cook until aromatic and just barely golden, but not browned, all over.

Meanwhile, place the stock, creamer, miso, and pepper in your blender, and briefly blitz to combine. Then, with the motor running on low, slowly sprinkle Vegg powder into the center of the canister to incorporate. If using a Vita-Mix, aim for the center of the vortex to prevent it from merely sticking to the sides and clumping.

Gently pour Vegg mixture into the pan of aromatics, whisking to incorporate. Continue cooking, stirring periodically, until the sauce thickens and bubbles break rapidly on the surface.

Pour the hot sauce over the cooked pasta, toss to coat, and portion out onto plates. Top with parsley and your "bacon" of choice, and serve immediately. It will continue to thicken as it cools, and doesn't make for great leftovers. The noodles will glue themselves together after a trip to the fridge, so enjoy right away.

Maitake & Baby Kale Pasta

By: Cobi Kim
www.veggietorials.com

Makes 2-4 Servings

Ingredients for the sauce:
10 oz. dry spaghetti, cooked
6 cups baby kale (washed and dried)
2 Tbs. + 3 Tbs. olive oil
1 yellow onion, diced
4 cloves garlic, minced
1 cup prepared Vegg
1+1/2 cup non-dairy milk
3 Tbs. flour
2 Tbs. garlic, onion powder, chives
seasoning blend
1/4 cup nutritional yeast
1/4 cup vegan bacon bits
salt and pepper to taste
1 large pot for cooking pasta
1 large saute pan to make sauce

For the mushrooms:
2 cups maitake mushrooms
1 Tbs. olive oil
salt and pepper
2 sprigs thyme

For the sauce: Cook pasta until al dente, drain, set aside. Heat 2 Tbs. olive oil in saucepan and cook onions until caramelized. Add garlic and cook for 2 minutes.

Remove onions and garlic from pan, set aside. Heat remaining 3 Tbs. of olive oil on med high heat in the same pan and add flour to create a roux. Add non-dairy milk and Vegg and whisk until smooth. Mix in seasoning, salt and pepper, nutritional yeast and cooked onions/garlic. Add baby kale to the sauce and mix until wilted.

Toss pasta with sauce. Top with mushrooms and bacon bits. Serve immediately.

For the mushrooms: Clean and rough chop maitake mushrooms. Heat olive oil in small pan and cook mushrooms and thyme over med high heat for 4 minutes. Season with salt and pepper.

Hard Boiled Veggs

By: Karolina Tegelaar
www.kakboken.com

Ingredients for yolk:
3/4 cups water
1/2 tsp. agar agar powder (not flakes)
1/4 tsp. black salt
4 tsp. Vegg powder
1/4 tsp. turmeric (optional)

For white:
1 cup soy cream (unflavored)
1+1/8 cups silken tofu
2 tsp. black salt
2 Tbsp. agar agar powder (not flakes)

For yolk: Bring 3/4 cups water to a boil with 1/2 tsp. agar agar powder (not flakes). Take it from the stove and stir in 4 tsp.of Vegg powder and 1/4 tsp. of black salt (Optionally add food coloring or a bit of turmeric if you want it to be a bit more yellow).

For white: Blend together soy cream, tofu, black salt and agar agar powder in a pot so that there are no tofu pieces left. Bring it to a boil so that the agar agar dissolves and pour it into the egg molds (I use jello molds). If you have egg molds you can fill half the mold with egg white, insert a round yolk made from the firm yolk mixture, close the mold and pour in egg white until it is full.

Chill and serve.

Panko Crusted Tofu Medallions

By: Cobi Kim
www.veggietorials.com

Prep: 1 hour | Cook: 30 minutes

Ingredients for the tofu medallions:
1 block organic tofu (firm or extra firm)
1 cup panko mixed with 3-4 Tbs.
curry seasoning
1 cup prepared Vegg yolk
oil for frying

For the noodles:
1 pkg. shirataki noodles
1 tsp. sesame oil
1 tsp. chili oil
1 Tbs. rice vinegar
1 Tbs. agave nectar
1 Tbs. nama shoyu
1 small carrot, julienned
2 cups kale, finely chopped, massaged with
a drizzle of oil and a big pinch of sea salt
sesame seeds, green onions for garnish

For the Tofu: Drain water and remove tofu from pkg. Press excess water out of tofu using your preferred method.

Cut pressed tofu into medallion shapes. Dip tofu into Vegg mixture and then dredge in panko and spice mix. Coat evenly.

Heat oil in a pan on the stove and pan fry medallions for about 2 minutes on the top and bottom. Fry the medallions on the sides to get a nice crispy crust.

For the Noodles: Prepare noodles according to directions on the pkg. Mix sesame oil, chili oil, agave, shoyu and rice vinegar in a small bowl. Add sauce to noodles after they have been drained and rinsed. Toss with wilted kale and top with carrots, sesame seeds and green onions. Plate with tofu medallions.

Serve immediately. The noodles can be kept in an airtight container for up to 2 days but the tofu medallions are best eaten right after preparation.

Vegan Okonomiyaki

By: Cobi Kim
www.veggietorials.com

Makes 2 servings

Ingredients for the pancake:
1 cup cake flour (or mix 3/4 cup + 2 Tbs.
all-purpose flour with 2 Tbs. cornstarch)
1/2 tsp. baking powder
1 Tbs. dulse (optional)
3/4 cup water or kombu dashi
4 Tbs. prepared Vegg
2 vegan prawns, chopped
1/2 cup vegan bacon bits
1 cup thinly sliced cabbage
1/2 cup green onions, chopped

For the spicy mayo:
1/2 cup vegan mayo
1 Tbs. mirin
1 Tbs. hot sauce

For the okonomiyaki sauce:
mix 2 Tbs. ketchup + 2 Tbs. vegan
worcestershire sauce
(or coconut aminos for soy-free)

For garnish:
green onions, sesame seeds,
pickled ginger, seaweed rice seasoning,
seaweed powder

Combine cake flour, dulse and baking powder in a large bowl. Mix in water (or dashi) and Vegg until smooth. Add cabbage, green onions, prawns and bacony bits.

Heat a non stick skillet over high heat. Pour half of the mixture into the pan and form into a pancake. Cover and cook for 2 minutes. Flip and cook for another 2 minutes. Flip one last time for 3 minutes.

Brush with okonomiyaki sauce and garnish with spicy mayo, seaweed, rice seasoning, sesame seeds, pickled ginger and green onions.

Vegg Spinach Quiche

By: Rocky Shepheard
www.thevegg.com

Ingredients:

1 lb. Scrambled Vegg (see page 11)
2 cups chopped fresh baby spinach, packed
vegan shredded cheddar
1 9" pie crust
salt and pepper to taste

Distribute thawed scrambled Vegg and spinach into premade pie crust.

Bake at 350F for approximately 45 minutes (check often to make sure crust does not burn).

Remove from oven and add vegan cheddar on top. Broil until vegan cheese melts.

Remove let stand 20 minutes and serve.

Potato Salad Plus

By: Cobi Kim; www.veggietorials.com

Prep: 15 minutes | Cook: 40 minutes
Serves 12

Ingredients:

6-8 large russet potatoes, skin on
1 cup chopped celery or water chestnuts
1/4 cup chopped red onion
1/2 cup sun dried tomatoes, chopped
1/4 cup roasted red bell peppers
3 Tbs. Italian parsley, finely chopped
1/2 cup vegan mayonnaise
1/2 cup prepared Vegg
1 Tbs. mustard powder
3 Tbs. sweet pickle relish
1 tsp. celery salt
1 Tbs. dill
2 Tbs. citrus garlic seasoning blend
salt and pepper

Boil the potatoes with the skin on until easily pierced with a fork (about 30-40 minutes). Remove from heat, drain and cool potatoes. Peel off skins and cut into bite sized cubes. Add to a large bowl with all of the veggie ingredients.

Mix all of the ingredients for the dressing. Use more of Vegg mixture for a creamier taste. Adjust seasonings and add salt and pepper to taste.

Pour the dressing over the potatoes and veggies. Mix until potatoes are well coated. Garnish with heirloom grape tomatoes, spicy pickled green beans or vegan bacon bits.

Indian Quinoa, Pea & Potato Croquettes

By: Nancy Montuari Stein
www.ordinaryvegan.net

Makes 12-15

Ingredients:

2 large potatoes, boiled, peeled and mashed
1 cup cooked quinoa
1/2 cup peas (fresh or frozen)
steam briefly if frozen
1/4 cup fresh coriander leaves, chopped
2 tsp. ground cumin
1 tsp. garam masala
2 cloves of garlic, finely chopped
1/4 cup of bread crumbs
1 Tbs. prepared Vegg
salt and pepper to taste
a few Tbs. olive oil for frying

Heat a Tbs. oil on medium heat in a frying pan. Add garlic and peas. Saute for a minute until soft and peas cooked. Remove from heat and put into a large bowl. Wipe pan clean with paper towel.

Add the potatoes, quinoa, coriander, salt, pepper, cumin and garam masala, bread crumbs and Vegg to the garlic and peas. Mix well and form into slightly flattened oblong croquettes.

Add a Tbs. of oil in the frying pan, increase heat to medium-high. When oil is hot, add 4-5 croquettes to the pan depending on the size and cook each side for about four minutes, flipping very gently until very brown on both sides. They can also be baked with a light spray of olive oil in a pre-heated oven for 10-15 minutes at 375F until browned.

Repeat with remaining croquettes. Serve hot with spicy dipping sauce.

Southern Style Potato Salad

By: Yolanda Batts

Makes 6 servings

Ingredients:

5-6 medium potatoes
1+1/2 cups of vegan mayonnaise
1+1/2 tsp. yellow mustard
1/2 cup prepared Vegg
1/3 cup India relish
1/2 cup chopped celery hearts
1/2 cup chopped red onion
1/2 cup chopped carrots, blanched
1 Tbs. finely chopped parsley
1 tsp. onion powder
1 tsp. garlic powder
1/2 tsp. celery seeds
1 tsp. organic sugar
salt and pepper to taste
paprika

Boil potatoes (with skins on) in a large pot until fork tender (approx. 20-30 minutes).

While the potatoes are boiling, chop the vegetables (celery hearts, red onion, carrots, and parsley). After chopping the vegetables, in separate bowl, combine the vegan mayonnaise, Vegg, India relish, yellow mustard, onion powder, garlic powder, celery seeds, and sugar. (This is the dressing for the potato salad).

In a separate small pot, blanch the carrots in boiling water until slightly tender (approx. 3-5 minutes). Drain and set aside.

When the potatoes are done, drain and let cool to room temperature then remove the skins and cut into cubes.

Lightly salt the potatoes then add all chopped vegetables. Lightly mix the potatoes and vegetables together being careful not to break up the potatoes. If they are breaking up immediately, they are probably overcooked—put them in the refrigerator for approx. 20 minutes to firm up.

Gently fold in the dressing, combining all ingredients. Add salt and pepper to taste. Garnish with paprika.

Spaghetti alla Carbonara

By: Monika Soria Caruso
www.windycityvegan.wordpress.com

Serves 3-4 as a main course

Ingredients:
1/2 lb. best quality gluten free spaghetti
1+1/2 tsp. Vegg powder + 6 Tbs. water
4 slices vegan bacon
a few generous pinches of vegan parmesan
salt and pepper to taste
a few sprigs of parsley, minced

Line prep: Put on a large, deep pot of liberally salted water to boil. Get your skillet ready to heat up your vegan bacon. Mince your parsely and grind your parm, then set both aside for later.

Make your Vegg: It is very important to blend it well for several seconds, with an actual blender of some sort. Whisking will not suffice! I used my immersion blender and combined 1+1/2 tsp. Vegg powder with 6 Tbs. water and blended on high for 30 plus seconds. If you don't have an immersion blender, there are directions on the package for mixing up the entire packet in a standard blender, as well as how to store it.

Make your vegan bacon: Time this so that your vegan bacon is finished cooking right before you drain the pasta. Cut each strip of cooked vegan bacon into 1/2" pieces and leave in the skillet to stay warm.

Compose your dish: Drain your pasta and immediately transfer to a large bowl. Drizzle with The Vegg; toss to coat evenly. Add a couple of Tbs. of vegan parm, salt, and a few generous turns of the pepper mill; toss again to coat evenly. Taste and season again if needed. Add the vegan bacon and toss one more time. Plate out the individual portions and top each with an additional pinch of vegan parm and minced parsley.

53

Summer Veggie Casserole

By: Jackie Sobon
www.vegancuts.com

Serves: 2-3
Prep: 20 minutes | Cook Time: 45 minutes

Ingredients:

1 cup zucchini, grated
1 cup button mushrooms, diced
1 cup white onion, diced
1/2 cup carrot, grated
1 cup kale, chopped, deribbed,
and loosely-packed
8 tsp. Vegg powder
2 cups water
1/3 tsp. salt
1/4 tsp. black pepper
1 cup panko crumbs, + an extra 1/4 cup for topping

Preheat the oven to 375F. Press the moisture out of the shredded zucchini with a clean cloth.

Place the zucchini, mushrooms, white onion, carrot, and kale into a large bowl, toss together with a fork.

In a blender, purée Vegg powder and water together on high until the consistency is even and there are no clumps.

Pour Vegg mixture over the veggies, season them with salt and pepper and start incorporating the panko crumbs into the veggie mixture.

Make sure, again, that the consistency is even. Carefully place the casserole mixture into 2-3 4" casserole dishes, or spread it out in an 8"x8" casserole dish.

Sprinkle the remaining panko crumbs over the top and bake for 45 minutes or until the veggie mixture isn't soupy or watery.

Once it's done baking, let it cool 5-10 minutes before serving.

Vegg Tempura

By: Monica Vereau Trzaska

Ingredients:

1 Tbs. of Vegg prepared
with 1/4 cup of water
1/2 cup unbleached flour
1/2 cup ice cold water
2 green onions
1/2 yellow spicy chile (or any chile)
1 dash of baking soda
salt and pepper (to taste)
2 cubes of ice

Blend all the ingredients very well using a food processor, for about 2 minutes.

Put the tempura in a bowl. Use immediately to coat and deep fry any food item (best with vegetables) in very hot oil. Frying time takes only seconds. Vegg gives the tempura a nice golden finish.

You can also use it on vegan fish fillets or tofu.

Vegg Potato Rose

By: Kristel De Geest
www.tofuparty.wordpress.com

Ingredients:
2 large potatoes
1/3 cup + 1 Tbs. non-dairy milk
2 Tbs. vegan margarine
1/2 cup prepared Vegg

Preheat the oven to 400F.

Peel the potatoes and boil them for about 20 minutes until thoroughly cooked.

Mash them very well. There shouldn't be any lumps left. Stir in non-dairy milk and margarine. Mix very well. Let it cool.

Prepare Vegg and stir into the cooled mash. Pour the purée into a pastry or plastic bag.

Grease a baking pan with margarine and make roses on the pan. (Or use baking paper or a silicon mat.)

Slide it in the middle of the oven and bake the roses for about 20 minutes, or until they brown a bit.

Baked Frittata

By: Chris Dixon; www.veganoo.net

Ingredients vegetables:
5-6 medium potatoes, cut in 1 in. chunks
2 medium onions, coarsely chopped
1/2 cup green beans
2/3 cup red or orange pepper
4 Tbs. good olive oil
2 Tbs. chopped fresh herbs: rosemary, thyme, chives

Eggy mix:
2-1/2 cups firm silken tofu (12 oz.)
1 cup cold water
6 Tbs. arrowroot powder or cornstarch
2 Tbs. Vegg powder
2 Tbs. rapeseed oil (canola)

2 cloves garlic, crushed
1/3 tsp. salt
1/4 tsp. pepper

Mix the vegetables, herbs and olive oil in a 9" square baking dish. Roast in the oven at 360F for 30 minutes

In a blender mix Vegg powder with the water until smooth, then blend in the remaining ingredients.

Pour the eggy mix over the roasted vegetables and bake at 360F for 30-40 minutes. Allow to cool a little, cut and serve.

The quantity of arrowroot given won't set the frittata very firmly...it will be slightly saucy. Add a little more if you want it to set.

Vegg Carbonara

By: Amy Krell
www.TheComfortingVegan.Blogspot.com

Ingredients:

1 lb. dry spaghetti
3 Tbs. extra-virgin olive oil
4 oz. vegan bacon, cubed or
sliced into small strips
4 garlic cloves, finely chopped
1/4 cup prepared Vegg
1 cup grated vegan cheese,
jack or mozzarella flavor
1 Tbs. vegan parmesan cheese, for serving
salt and freshly ground black pepper
1 handful fresh flat-leaf parsley, chopped

Prepare the sauce while the pasta is cooking to ensure that the spaghetti will be hot and ready when the sauce is finished; it is very important that the pasta is hot when adding Vegg mixture, so that the heat of the pasta melts the cheese in the sauce.

Bring a large pot of salted water to a boil, add the pasta and cook for 8-10 minutes or until tender yet firm (or "al dente").

Drain the pasta well, reserving 1/2 cup of the hot starchy cooking water to use in the sauce if you wish.

Meanwhile, heat the olive oil in a deep skillet over medium flame. Add the vegan bacon and saute for about 5 minutes, or until the vegan bacon is crisp.

Toss the garlic into the vegan bacon and saute for less than 1 minute to soften.

Add the hot, drained spaghetti to the pan and toss for 2 minutes to coat the strands in the vegan bacon.

Beat Vegg and vegan cheese together in a mixing bowl, stirring well. Remove the pan from the heat and pour The Vegg/cheese mixture onto the pasta, toss until Vegg mixture mixes with the pasta. Thin out the sauce with a bit of the reserved pasta water, until it reaches desired consistency.

Season the carbonara with several turns of freshly ground black pepper and taste for salt.

Mound the spaghetti carbonara into warm serving bowls and garnish with chopped parsley and vegan parmesan.

Loco Moco

By: Cobi Kim; www.veggietorials.com

Serves 4

Ingredients for the gravy:
2 Tbs. vegan margarine
2 Tbs. flour*
1+1/2 Tbs. no-chicken bouillon
2 cups hot water
1 Tbs. ketchup
1 tsp. vegan Worcestershire sauce
1-2 tsp. soy sauce or tamari (gluten-free)
black pepper

Substitute arrowroot powder or the thickener of your choice for gluten-free option

For Vegg whites:
1/2 block silken (extra firm) tofu (6 oz.)
1/2 cup unsweetened coconut milk
1 Tbs. + 1 tsp. sweet rice flour
3 tsp. potato starch
1/2 tsp. truffle salt*
food processor or blender
omelet pan

Truffle salt will give the whites a very convincing flavor. Truffles are similar to mushrooms and bring subtle umami quality to the whites. You can experiment with different types of salt and adjust to your taste.

For Vegg yolk:
2 Tbs. Vegg
1+1/4 cup filtered water
food processor or blender

For spherified Vegg yolk:
5 grams food grade calcium chloride
500 ml room temperature filtered water
glass with small diameter
waterbath

For the gravy: Heat margarine and flour in a pan on medium heat until the flour becomes a golden tan color, about 3-5 minutes, stirring constantly. Dissolve bouillon in hot water to make broth. Add 1 cup of broth slowly to the pan. Whisk until smooth and no lumps. Add more broth if necessary to achieve desired thickness. Mix in ketchup, Worcestershire, soy sauce and black pepper. Adjust seasonings to taste.

For Vegg whites: Combine all ingredients in food processor. Blend until smooth and creamy. Mist omelet pan lightly with oil. Heat on med high. Spoon 2 Tbs. of the tofu mixture into the pan and spread in an even layer. Cook on high heat for 45 seconds, then drop down to medium. When edges start to look translucent and form air bubbles, they are cooked. Approx. 2 minutes. Flip and cook for 2 minutes. Do not over cook or they will look too dark.

For Vegg Yolk: Follow spherification directions on page 8.

**The gravy and fried Vegg will be placed over a vegan burger sitting on top of a bed of rice.

Chewy Crisp Banana Cookies

By: Claire Risley

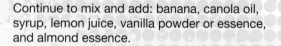

Ingredients:

2 small ripe bananas
1/4 cup water
1 cup coconut milk
2 tsp. Vegg powder
4 tsp. ground flax seed
1/2 cup canola oil
1 lemon, juiced
1 tsp. vanilla powder or essence
3 drops almond essence
3/4 cup syrup or agave
1 cup white flour
1 cup wholemeal flour
1/2 tsp. allspice
1 tsp. cinnamon
1 tsp. baking powder
1 cup oats
2 cups puffed rice
1 bar vegan chocolate (dark or white)

Set oven to 350F.

Put grease proof paper (parchment paper) on 2 baking trays.

Mash 2 small bananas.

Put the water, coconut milk, Vegg and flax seed into mixer and mix on slow for 10 seconds.

Continue to mix and add: banana, canola oil, syrup, lemon juice, vanilla powder or essence, and almond essence.

When it's blended, scrape into mixing bowl you mashed bananas in and sift in flours, allspice, cinnamon, baking powder and MIX VERY WELL.

Fold in oats well, and lastly 2 cups puffed rice, and spoon onto your lined trays, about 1 Tbs. for each cookie, at about 1" thickness.

Bake for 15 minutes.

Meanwhile melt chocolate pieces (in microwave or bain marie). If microwaving, check every 30 seconds and stir well (takes about 2 minutes of microwave time). It's best to have the chocolate not quite melted. It continues to melt after it's taken out if stirred.

Remove cookies from oven when browning on outside, drizzle melted chocolate over them then let cookies cool.

Date Nut Bread

By: Sandy DeFino; www.thevegg.com

Ingredients:

1 cup chopped pitted dates
3/4 cup boiling water
1/4 cup vegan margarine
1+1/2 cup flour
1+1/2 tsp. baking soda
1 tsp. salt
1/4 cup prepared Vegg
1 tsp. vanilla
3/4 cup sugar
3 Tbs. organic brown rice syrup
3/4 cup chopped walnuts

In a large bowl, combine dates, vegan margarine and water. Let stand 15 minutes.

Preheat oven to 350F.

Combine flour, baking soda, salt and set aside.

Add The Vegg, vanilla, sugar and syrup to date mixture and mix well. Stir in nuts and flour until just combined.

Pour into a greased 9"x 5" loaf pan.
Bake for 55-65 min.

Sunflower Seed Chocolate Cookies

By: Ginny McMeans
www.theveganinthefreezer.com

Ingredients:

2+1/2 cup whole wheat pastry flour
3 Tbs. prepared Vegg
3/4 tsp. baking soda
1/2 tsp. baking powder
1/2 tsp. salt
1 cup vegan margarine, softened
3/4 cup firmly packed brown sugar
2 Tbs. granulated beet sugar
1 tsp. vanilla extract
10 oz. chocolate chips
5 oz. shelled sunflower seeds

Lightly grease baking sheets for baking.

Sift together the flour, baking powder, baking soda and salt and set aside.

In a large bowl cream together the margarine and sugars until it is light and fluffy. (This will take a little while—just be patient.) Add the prepared Vegg mixture and vanilla and mix well.

Gradually add dry mixture to wet and mix until incorporated. Add chocolate chips and sunflower seeds and mix well.

Drop by teaspoonsful onto the prepared cookie sheets about 2-3 inches apart. Flatten the tops slightly.

Bake at 375F for 8-9 minutes.

After they have cooled keep them in a cool dry place or the refrigerator or the freezer.

Gluten-Free Lemon Bars

By: Lindsay Ray; www.arohanuiveganlove.wordpress.com

Ingredients:
1/3 cup vegan margarine
2/3 cup raw vegan sugar
1/2 cup prepared Vegg
1+1/4 cup gluten-free flour
1+1/2 tsp. baking powder
1/8 tsp. Himalayan salt
1/3 cup almond milk
1/2 tsp. vanilla extract
Depending on taste and the lemons...
1+1/2 tsp. grated lemon peel
1/4 cup juice of fresh lemons

Cream margarine and sugar

Whisk in Vegg mix, then add the rest of the ingredients.

Pour in small loaf greased pan and bake approx. 40 minutes at 350F.

Mocha Tofu Cheesecake

By: Richard Notali-Rombach

Ingredients:
8 oz. firm tofu
1 pkg. or about 12 oz. firm silken tofu
1/4 cup cashew butter (you can use more if you want a richer cheesecake)
1/2 cup prepared Vegg
1 cup sugar or alternative
1/4 cup strong espresso coffee
1/4 cup vegan chocolate chips melted
2 tsp. vanilla
2 Tbs. starch

Topping:
2/3 cup vegan chocolate chips
1/3 scant cup vegan cream alternative

Blend or process all cheesecake ingredients until smooth and creamy.

Pour into well greased 7" spring form pan or deep pie pan. You can use a larger spring form but it will be shallower. You can also use a prebaked bottom crust of your choice if you choose but I prefer mine without a crust.

Cover top of spring form pan with tin foil.

Bake at 350F for one hour.

**You may have to adjust baking time depending on your oven or if you increase recipe size. Convection ovens will give a more even heat. You can also use a food thermometer to check center temperature. It should be around 140F. Make sure tip of thermometer does not touch bottom of pan.*

**For pressure cooker: Fold a dish towel and place in bottom of pressure cooker. Pour in 3 cups of water. Place spring form pan on top of towel. Cook on rice setting for 30 minutes. After cooking allow pressure cooker to vent steam on its own.*

For Topping: Melt chocolate in vegan cream substitute. Spread on top of tofu cheesecake.

Let cool thoroughly and place in refrigerator. Serve and enjoy.

**A note about pressure cooking. Pressure cooking is a wonderful way to both cook and bake, using less energy without heating up the kitchen in warm weather. It is a great way to cook tofu cheesecakes as it cooks without drying out the top of the tofu cheesecake like traditional baking does.*

Mom's Sour Cream Coffee Cake

By: Stacy Di-Lin
www.veganfatty.com

Ingredients:
1/2 cup walnuts, finely chopped
1+1/2 tsp. ground cinnamon
3/4 cup sugar
3/4 cup vegan margarine
1+1/4 cups sugar
1+1/2 cups vegan sour cream
1+1/2 tsp. vanilla extract
1/2 cup + 2 Tbs. of prepared Vegg
3 cups all+purpose flour
1+1/2 tsp. baking powder
1+1/2 tsp. of baking soda

Preheat oven to 350F. Grease a 10" tube (bundt) pan.

In small bowl combine walnuts, cinnamon, and 3/4 cup sugar.

In large bowl, with mixer at medium speed, beat vegan margarine with 1+1/4 cup sugar until light and fluffy. Beat in vegan sour cream, vanilla, and Vegg. In separate bowl, combine flour with baking powder and baking soda.

Add dry ingredients to wet, increasing speed and beating for 3 minutes, scraping sides of bowl.

Spread half of batter into pan and sprinkle with half of nut mixture. Spread evenly with remaining batter then sprinkle remainder of sugar mixture on top.

Bake 60-65 minutes, until toothpick comes out clean and cake pulls away from side of pan.

Southern Red Velvet Brownies

By: Gwendolyn Mathers
www.cok.net

Ingredients:

1+1/4 cup all+purpose flour
1 cup beet purée
1/2 scant cup vegan margarine
1/2 cup evaporated cane sugar
1/2 cup cocoa powder
1/2 cup prepared Vegg
1 Tbs. vanilla
1 Tbs. lemon juice to keep color brighter
(optional)
1 Tbs. baking powder
1/4 tsp. salt

Cream Cheese Frosting:

6 oz. vegan cream cheese
1 Tbs. vegan margarine
1+1/2 cup powdered sugar
1 tsp. vanilla extract (optional)

Preheat the oven to 350F.

Mix the flour, baking powder, and salt. Set aside.

Cream the margarine and sugar, then add the cocoa, beets, vanilla, and lemon juice if using.

Blend or process Vegg according to package to make a half cup and add to the wet mixture.

Slowly add the flour mixture and stir just until no lumps appear.

Pour the batter into a greased or parchment paper lined 8"x8" pan and bake for 40 minutes or until a tooth pick inserted into the center comes out clean.

Allow to cool. Frost before removing from pan and cut into bars.

Frosting: Beat all ingredients with a mixer until smooth and creamy. Chill for at least 30 minutes to thicken before frosting.

Add more powdered sugar for a sweeter taste or thicker consistency.

Spiced Persimmon Creme Brulee

By: Steffi DeRobertis
www.dontfearthevegan.com

Ingredients for spiced persimmons:
4 peeled fuyu persimmons with tops cut off
enough water to cover
1 vanilla bean, split and scraped
3 whole peppercorns
3 cloves
1 cinnamon stick
1 1" piece of ginger root, peeled
and cut in thirds
2 Tbs. maple syrup

For pudding:
1 cup cashews, soaked for 8 hours
1 cup liquid reserved from persimmons
4 spiced persimmons, peeled (recipe above)
1 tsp. Vegg powder
1 Tbs. agar flakes
2 Tbs. maple syrup
1/2 cup brown sugar
1/3 cup white chocolate chips (optional)
1/4 cup raw sugar

In a medium size pot with a lid place the persimmons on the bottom, so that they are sitting next to each other and not on top of each other. Cover completely with water. Split and scrape the vanilla bean and add both the scrapings and the bean itself to the water.

Add all remaining "spiced persimmon" ingredients. Leaving the pot uncovered, bring to boil. Once it begins to boil reduce heat to simmer, cover, and cook for thirty minutes.

Strain persimmons reserving one cup of liquid. Set aside to cool.

Pulverize cashews in blender with 3/4 cups persimmon liquid until smooth and creamy. Add spiced persimmons, Vegg powder, agar, maple syrup and brown sugar, pouring remaining 1/4 cup persimmon liquid on top. Blend until smooth.

Pour mixture into a saucepan and cook on low, stirring constantly until all air bubbles are gone, about 15 minutes. Do not let it boil. Pour into ramekins. Refrigerate until completely cooled (or chill overnight.)

Before serving sprinkle raw sugar over the entire top, place a few optional white chocolate chips in the center, and brown the sugar with a blowtorch. Serve.

Spiced Vegg Nog

By: Kaycee Bassett; www.veganmachine.com

Ingredients:
2 cups soy or almond milk
2 cups vegan creamer
1/2 cup prepared Vegg
(1/2 cup water, 2 tsp. Vegg, blended)
2/3 cup sugar
1 tsp. vanilla extract
1/2 tsp. cinnamon
1/4 tsp. nutmeg
rum (optional, to your liking)

In a small pot heat your soy or almond milk and sugar until sugar is dissolved.

Once dissolved, add the rest of your ingredients besides creamer and rum.

Heat while stirring frequently for 20-25 minutes.

Stir in creamer. If you are adding rum to your nog, add right before serving. Garnish with more nutmeg. Vegg Nog can be served warm or cold!

Tiramisu Cupcakes

By: Matthew Calverley
www.vegan-heartland.com

Ingredients:
1+3/4 cups all+purpose flour
1+1/4 tsp. baking powder
1/2 tsp. salt
1/3 cup non+dairy milk
1 tsp. vanilla
3 tsp. of Vegg blended with
3/4 cup non+dairy milk
1+1/2 cup sugar
6 Tbs. vegan shortening

Frosting:
1+1/4 cup powdered sugar
1+1/2 cups vegan cream cheese
at room temp
unsweetened cocoa powder (for dusting)

Glaze:
1/2 cup brewed coffee
3 Tbs. coffee liqueur
6 Tbs. sugar

Preheat the oven to 325F. Sift together the flour, baking powder, and salt in a bowl. Set aside.

In a small bowl whisk together the non-dairy milk and vanilla. Set aside.

In a blender or food processor mix together the 3 tsp. of Vegg powder and 3/4 cup non-dairy milk.

Pour Vegg mixture into a large bowl. Whisk in the sugar until well combined then add the vegan shortening. Mix until light and fluffy.

Fold dry ingredients into Vegg mixture in three stages to allow for proper mixing. Once the dry ingredients are properly mixed into the wet, add the non-dairy milk and vanilla. Stir until just combined. Divide the batter into a lined or greased cupcake pan filling each liner about 3/4 of the way full. Bake at 325F for 18-20 minutes until golden brown. Cool on wire rack before applying glaze.

Glaze: Combine the coffee, coffee liqueur, and sugar. Whisk together until the sugar has dissolved. Once the cupcakes have cooled slightly poke the tops of each cake with a wooden skewer 4-5 times. Brush the glaze on top of each cupcake 5-6 times.

Frosting: In a medium sized bowl blend the cream cheese and powdered sugar together until well combined and the frosting is light and fluffy. Transfer the frosting into a piping bag and top each cupcake with the frosting. Lightly dust each cupcake with cocoa powder or top with shaved chocolate! Refrigerate until you're ready to serve!

Pots O' Chocolate

By: Lisa Petr

Makes 8 - 10 dessert glasses

Ingredients:

**12 oz. dark chocolate or semi-sweet
bars or chips (broken into pieces)
1/2 cup prepared Vegg
2 tsp. real vanilla extract
a pinch of salt
1 cup chocolate or vanilla almond milk
1/4 cup liquid sweetener**

Place the broken up chocolate in a blender.
Add The Vegg, the vanilla and salt. Pulse five
times. Heat the almond milk until very hot (I used
my microwave) and pour into blender. Blend it
until smooth. It will be very, very thick.

Taste the mixture and add sweetener to
accomodate your taste. Pour the mixture into
small glasses or bowls. Let set 30 minutes either
in the fridge or on the counter. Top with a dollop
of coconut cream, chocolate shavings or a couple
of ripe berries.

Options: You could add any liqueur to this mixture
to flavor it. You can use 1/8 tsp. peppermint
extract in place of the vanilla. You can use a
flavored chocolate. You can replace the almond
milk with strong coffee if you want a mocha flavor.

It will freeze well, just allow to thaw in fridge for a
day or more before serving. It will keep in fridge
for about a week.

Vegg Nog Pie

By: Sandy DeFino
www.thevegg.com

Ingredients:
pie crust
1 pkg. firm silken tofu
1/2 cup soaked raw cashews
(soaked 4-6 hrs and drained)
1/4 cup sugar or sweetener of your choice
1 cup prepared Vegg
1 tsp. nutmeg
1 tsp. vanilla
1 cup almond milk
1 tsp. agar-agar powder

Prebake a pie crust at 400F for 14 minutes (ours was frozen, but homemade should work too).

In a food processor or blender, combine tofu, cashews, sugar, Vegg, nutmeg and vanilla. Stopping to scrape the sides as necessary, combine until creamy.

Bring almond milk to a boil, whisk in agar-agar powder and continue to whisk as the mixture boils for 4-5 minutes.

Add the almond milk mixture to the mixture in the food processor and run it to incorporate everything into a thick, creamy filling.

Pour the filling into your prepared pie crust and refrigerate for several hours.

Banana Cream Meringue Pie

By: Sean Friend

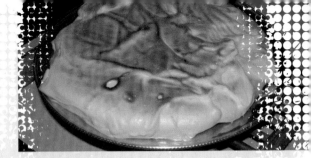

Ingredients:
9" pie shell, baked
3 cups soy milk
3/4 cup white sugar
1/3 cup all-purpose flour
1/4 tsp. salt
1/4 cup prepared Vegg
1/2 tsp. ground flax seed
2 Tbs. vegan margarine
1 tsp. vanilla
1-2 bananas

For the meringue:
3/4 cup water
1/4 cup wheat starch (corn starch wlll work)
1 tsp. xanthan gum
2 Tbs. soy protein isolate
1/4 tsp. cream of tartar
1 cup white sugar
3/4 tsp. vanilla extract

Have baked 9" pie shell ready.

In a large saucepan, scald the soy milk.

In another saucepan, combine the sugar, flour and salt; gradually stir in the scalded soy milk over medium heat, stirring constantly. Cook until thickened. Cover and, stirring occasionally, cook for 2 minutes longer.

In a small bowl, have the Vegg slightly beaten with the flax seed, ready; stir a small amount of the hot mixture into beaten Vegg; when thoroughly combined, stir into hot mixture. Cook for 1 minute longer, stirring constantly. Remove from heat and blend in the vegan margarine and vanilla. Let sit until lukewarm.

Meanwhile, in a medium mixing bowl add the water, wheat starch, and xanthan gum, and beat for 1 minute. Add the soy protein isolate and beat for 2 more minutes. Add the cream of tartar and beat for 4 more minutes. Carefully sprinkle half the sugar into the mixture and continue to beat until incorporated (about 30 seconds). Add the vanilla extract. Reduce speed to the lowest setting on your mixer and slowly add the remaining sugar. Mix until just incorporated.

When your pudding mixture is lukewarm, slice bananas and scatter in pie shell; pour warm mixture over bananas. You can layer if you want to add more banana, but make sure there is pudding covering all of the banana slices.

Carefully spread the meringue on top of the pie. You can use the point of a spoon to dab at the top to create small peaks. Cool in the fridge for a couple of hours, until everything has solidified. If desired, put the pie under a broiler for just a couple of minutes to toast the top. Serve cold.

Lemon Curd

By: Sandy DeFino
www.thevegg.com

Ingredients:
zest of 2 lemons
juice of 2 lemons
1/3 cup sugar
1/4 cup prepared Vegg
1 Tbsp. cornstarch

Zest and juice two lemons. Heat the juice from two lemons in a small sauce pan.

Dissolve 1/3 cup sugar in the lemon juice. Stir in 1/4 cup of prepared Vegg. Stir in the lemon zest. Let simmer (on low) for 10-15 minutes.

Strain out the lemon zest and put most of the liquid back in the sauce pan (reserving 3 Tbsp. of the liquid to mix with the cornstarch in a separate container).

Whisk in liquid/cornstarch mixture into liquid in sauce pan. Heat (on medium) while whisking until mixture thickens to desired consistency.

Creme Brulee

By: Erin Wysocarski
www.olivesfordinner.com

Ingredients:
1 can of full+fat coconut milk
1/2 vanilla bean, scraped or
1 tsp. vanilla extract
1/2 tsp. agar powder
1+1/2 tsp. of Vegg powder
5+1/2 Tbs. water
1/4 cup superfine sugar
extra superfine sugar, for topping

Preheat oven to 325F. Combine the coconut milk, vanilla and agar in a small saucepan and heat over medium heat until it just starts to slightly boil, then dial the heat back to the lowest setting.

In a blender or mixer, combine Vegg powder with the water until well combined, about 15 seconds. Do not mix by hand or it will not work correctly. Then add in the sugar and blend again.

Pour Vegg mixture into the saucepan through a fine-mesh strainer. Whisk vigorously to combine. Keep over the heat for a minute or two so the sugar can dissolve. Turn off the heat and remove the mixture from the burner.

Create a water bath by placing two ramekins in a glass pyrex dish. Pour the mixture into the ramekins, then pour water into the glass pyrex dish until it comes up to about half the height of your ramekins.

Place it into the oven, ensuring that none of the water spills over into the ramekins. Bake for 30 minutes. Remove the ramekins from the water bath as soon as they are cool enough to handle. Cover the ramekins with saran wrap, making sure it does not come into contact with the mixture. Place in the refrigerator to set overnight.

When you are ready to serve the creme brulee, sprinkle about a Tbs. of the superfine sugar over the top. Using a butane torch, sweep the flame over the top until a golden caramel color is achieved. Serve immediately.

French Madelines

By: Lisa Petr

Ingredients:
1/4 cup all-purpose gluten free
or regular flour
3+1/2 Tbs. corn starch
1/4 cup ground almond flour/meal
1/3 cup The Vegg prepared per package
with water (or optionally almond milk)
9 Tbs. sugar
zest of 1/2 a lemon
1 tsp. vanilla extract or
1/2 tsp. almond extract

Mix all the ingredients together in a bowl.

Spoon into prepared Madeline pans (greased and floured) until 2/3 full.

Bake at 400F for 8 minutes.

They will fall after they are out of the oven but they taste lovely.

Cool completely in the pan.

Peanutbutter Bacon Chocolate Donuts

By: Mina Azarnoush
www.eatrun-love.blogspot.com

Ingredients:

1 cup all-purpose white flour
1/2 cup raw turbinado sugar
2 Tbs. cocoa powder
2 Tbs. fine instant coffee
1+1/2 tsp. baking powder
1/4 tsp. salt
2 heaping Tbs. unsweetened applesauce
2/3 cup vegan chocolate chips
1/2 cup soy milk
1/2 tsp. apple cider vinegar
(any light/white vinegar should work fine)
1/4 cup prepared Vegg
1/2 tsp. vanilla

Frosting and topping:

1+1/2 cup powdered sugar
1/3 cup smooth peanut butter
3 Tbs. non-dairy milk
vegan bacon bits (or you can bake tempeh
bacon if you want to be extra legit)

Pre-heat your oven to 350F.

In a large bowl mix together all the "dry"
ingredients, EXCEPT for the applesauce.
Reserve this for later.

In a small pot over low to medium heat, mix up
all of the "Wet" ingredients just until all of the
chocolate chips are melted and the mixture looks
even.

Slowly add in the liquid mixture to the "dry" bowl.
Mix for about 20 seconds and then add in the
applesauce.

Stir just until incorporated. Avoid stirring for too
long as this will make the dough too tough. The
dough should be sticky.

Using a small spoon if using a mini donut pan (If
you have a regular sized donut pan, use a large
spoon) plop down a dollop of the dough into the
molds. This part may get messy but it's okay.
Spread the dough into the mold until the mold is
filled and the little "hole" in the center of the mold
is exposed.

Bake in the oven for 13 minutes; the donuts
should bounce back when pressed gently.

Remove the donuts and let them cool in
the trays for a few minutes.

In order to remove the donuts, gently spin them
around individually while they are still in their
molds to ensure that they are not stuck. Then
remove them. Let them cool on a cooling rack
while preparing the glaze.

For glaze and topping: Cooled donuts in the
back. Glaze on the left, and bacon bits on the
right. Ready to begin assembling!

In a medium bowl pour out the bacon bits and
set aside.

In a small bowl mix together the peanut butter, sugar, and soy milk until even and smooth.

Pop this in the microwave for about 45 seconds so that it loosens up and is easier to pour.

Using a small spoon, gently pour this over the donuts like a glaze/frosting.

After letting the glaze set for a minute or two (it should not be runny, but should not be completely set). Dip the glazed portion of the donuts into the bowl of bacon bits. Set aside and let it set until you are ready to serve.

French Vanilla Ice Cream

By: Bryanna Clark Grogan; www.veganfeastkitchen.blogspot.com

Ingredients:
2 cups almond milk
2 Tbs. oil
3 tsp. premixed Vegg
1/2 cup light-colored unbleached
organic granulated sugar
1 tsp. pure vanilla extract or vanilla bean*
1/2 tsp. xanthan gum

Toppings:
I served the ice cream with grilled fresh
pineapple slices and some toasted
coconut flakes!

Combine all ingredients in a high speed blender or food processor. Blend until very smooth.

Chill the mixture thoroughly, pour into ice cream maker and follow manufacturer instructions.

**If you want to use a vanilla bean instead of vanilla extract, slit the vanilla pod lengthwise with a sharp knife tip. Scrape the sticky seeds out and add the pod and seeds to a pot with the almond milk and bring to a boil. Turn off heat and allow to cool in the refrigerator, then strain the milk before using in the recipe.